THE **100+** SERIES™

Reproducible Activities

MW00946208

Theme-Based
Vocabulary Builders

Grade 3

Published by Instructional Fair • TS Denison
an imprint of

Mc Graw Hill **Children's Publishing**

Editors: Linda Triemstra, Mary Hassinger

 Children's Publishing

Published by Instructional Fair • TS Denison
An imprint of McGraw-Hill Children's Publishing
Copyright © 2004 McGraw-Hill Children's Publishing

All Rights Reserved • Printed in the United States of America

Limited Reproduction Permission: Permission to duplicate these materials is limited to the person for whom they are purchased. Reproduction for an entire school or school district is unlawful and strictly prohibited.

Send all inquiries to:
McGraw-Hill Children's Publishing
3195 Wilson Drive NW
Grand Rapids, Michigan 49544

Theme-Based Vocabulary Builders—grade 3
ISBN: 0-7424-1933-9

1 2 3 4 5 6 7 8 9 MAL 09 08 07 06 05 04
The McGraw·Hill Companies

Table of Contents

Table of Contents

Table of Contents

Introduction

Theme-Based Vocabulary Builders is designed to introduce young readers to words in context. Each section of this book is based on a theme and contains pages that relate to each area of the curriculum: the arts, including sports; math; science; and social studies. A list of correlations to the standards follows on page 7.

Woven throughout the book are subthemes that can be expanded or emphasized. They include

Architecture—in Ancient Civilizations, Shapes, Color, and Light, Mexico

Deserts—in Australia, Mojave Desert State Parks, Mexico

Olympics—in Ancient Civilizations, Summer, and Winter

Patterns—in Australia, India, and Shapes, Color, and Light

Pottery—in Valles Caldera National Preserve, and Shapes, Color, and Light

Slavery—in Ancient Civilizations and Summer

Storytelling—in Australia and Valles Caldera National Preserve

In addition, this book is designed to give opportunities for enrichment. The pages about the arts, for example, could be enhanced by making available to students photos of well-known paintings or small pieces of stained glass. Teachers might also want to draw out similarities, such as those between Piet Mondrian and Frank Lloyd Wright.

Within each section of this book, the pages contain progressively more difficult material. This principle also holds true throughout the book, so teachers may wish to use some pages after material has been covered in class. Teachers will also want to have dictionaries available for students to use.

Standards Correlations

Arts

13, 25, 31, 32, 41, 45, 49, 51, 53, 55, 56, 59, 60, 63, 68, 72, 76, 82, 85, 95, 96, 104, 106, 112, 116

Math

15, 16, 17, 23, 33, 38–39, 46–47, 48, 50, 61, 62, 66, 73, 77, 78, 83, 89, 92, 98, 101, 109, 111, 115

Science

11, 12, 14, 19, 20, 24, 26, 27, 28, 29, 34, 35, 37, 42, 43, 54, 57, 58, 64, 67, 69, 74, 79, 81, 84, 86, 90, 91, 94, 97, 100, 102, 105, 107, 113, 114

Social studies

10, 18, 21, 22, 30, 36, 40, 44, 52, 65, 70, 71, 75, 80, 87, 88, 93, 99, 103, 108, 110, 117

Pretest/Posttest

1. A kind of stone is
       a. seed.
       b. marble.
       c. garlic.

2. A cylinder looks like
       a. a basket.
       b. a ball.
       c. a piece of pipe.

3. A kangaroo is an animal with
       a. skin.
       b. fur.
       c. feathers.

4. A flat area that is higher than the land around it is
       a. a cave.
       b. a plateau.
       c. a volcano.

5. A glacier is made of
       a. ice.
       b. rock.
       c. sand.

6. A theater is a place where
       a. people keep boats.
       b. people ride bikes.
       c. plays are given.

Pretest/Posttest

7. An octagon is
    a. a figure that has eight sides.
    b. a figure that has three sides.
    c. a figure that has five sides.

8. A very large area of land is
    a. an ocean.
    b. an island.
    c. a continent.

9. We weigh something like a stone in
    a. degrees.
    b. pounds.
    c. inches.

10. An animal that lives in a jungle is
    a. a seal.
    b. a moose.
    c. a jaguar.

11. An artist is a person who
    a. paints pictures.
    b. runs races.
    c. hunts animals.

12. An ocean is
    a. a small body of freshwater.
    b. water that flows between banks.
    c. a large body of saltwater.

Earth and Water

Directions: ─────────────────────

Use the Word Bank to name each place or thing.

┌───────────── **Word Bank** ─────────────┐

| ocean | glaciers | pond | marsh |
| stream | dunes | islands | beach |

└───────────────────────────────────────┘

1. Water that flows between banks is a _____ .

2. A _____ is an area of soft, wet land.

3. A small body of freshwater is a _____ .

4. A large body of water is a(n) _____ .

5. Small pieces of land surrounded by water are _____ .

6. Cape Cod was formed by the movement of _____ .

7. The sandy place by a large body of water is a _____ .

8. In this place, you will find piles of sand, called _____ .

In the Sea or on Land

Directions:

Use the Word Bank. Unscramble the names of the animals.

Word Bank

hawk	mouse	turtle	lobster
whale	snake	crab	salamander

1. **eahlw** _____

2. **seomu** _____

3. **wkah** _____

4. **barc** _____

5. **utrlte** _____

6. **aknes** _____

7. **lasmaredan** _____

8. **slreotb** _____

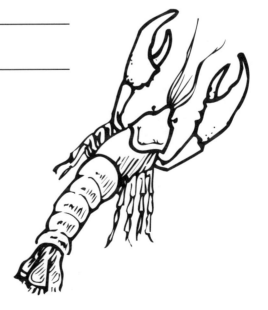

Science

Finding Homes

Directions: _____

Where does each animal live? Make a check in the correct column.

	land	water	both
1. whale			
2. mouse			
3. hawk			
4. crab			
5. turtle			
6. snake			
7. salamander			
8. lobster			

© McGraw-Hill Children's Publishing

0-7424-1933-9 *Theme-Based Vocabulary Builders*

Name _____ Date _____

Small Pictures

⳾Directions: ———————————————————

Use the Word Bank to fill in the blanks.

——————— **Word Bank** ———————

scrimshaw	images	folk art	endangered	
carve	ivory	resin	museums	whalers

1. Some men from Cape Cod and Nantucket were called _____ because they hunted whales.

2. To pass time, some men made pictures, or _____ , on whalebone.

3. Sometimes they made these pictures on tusks or _____ .

4. They would _____ the pictures into the whalebone.

5. This kind of art is called _____ .

6. It is _____ , a kind of art that parents teach their children to make.

7. Some old pieces of this art are in _____ or are owned by people in the artists' families.

8. People who make this art now use _____ instead of whalebone.

9. This is because some whales are _____ .

Useful Plants

⋛Directions: ──────────────────────────

Match the word in the left column with its meaning in the right column.

1. pine

   a. Some people eat this food at Thanksgiving.

2. holly

   b. This plant has small fruit that is used to make preserves.

3. beach plum

   c. This plant has hard wood that was sometimes used to make ships.

4. salt marsh rose

   d. This tall plant has nuts with smooth, hard shells.

5. cranberry

   e. This plant is one that people use in the winter holidays.

6. birch

   f. This tree is easy to find on Cape Cod.

7. hickory

   g. This plant has bark that peels easily.

8. oak

   h. This flower is found in soft, wet land.

Count 'em, Count 'em

Scientists who study animals, sometimes count the number of animals they find. This chart, or *table*, shows a count of three kinds of animals.

Animal numbers for two seasons (average)	Season			
	late summer	4	1	0
	mid-summer	4	1	1
	early summer	6	1	1
	late spring	3	1	1
		mouse	shrew	chipmunk

Animal

Directions:

Use the words in the Word Bank to name the parts of the chart shown.

— Word Bank —

Animals   Seasons   Number of animals for two seasons (average)

The part of the chart on the left side is a *label*. A label tells about some of the things in the chart.

The part of the table just above the top line is another *label*. It tells about other information in the table.

The *title* shown above is on the far left side of the table. The title tells what the table is about.

1. What is one label in this table? _____

2. What is the other label? _____

3. What is the title of this table? _____

Counting Mice

A scientist might want to look at the number of one kind of animal. A way to show those numbers is to make a graph like the one to the right.

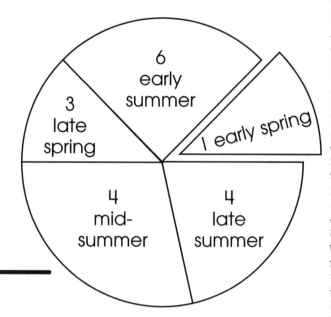

Number of mice by season

6 early summer

3 late spring

1 early spring

4 mid-summer

4 late summer

⋛Directions:

Use the Word Bank to fill in the blanks.

—— Word Bank ——

| segment | pie chart | circle | number | value |

1. This kind of graph is called a _____ graph.

2. Another name for this kind of graph is a _____ .

3. Each pie-shaped piece of the chart is a _____ .

4. How much each piece of the chart is worth is called the _____ .

Look at the chart to answer the questions below.

5. What is the title of the chart? _____

6. What is one label in the graph? _____

7. What is another label in the graph? _____

Finding Your Way Around

Directions:

Use the Word Bank to fill in the blanks.

Word Bank

intersection	map	symbol
intersect	location	grid

1. This picture is called a _____ .

2. This picture is drawn on a _____ , or a set of lines that cross each other.

3. Using this picture shows you how to find the place, or _____ , of the buildings.

4. You can name the avenues and streets that cross each other, or

   _____ .

5. Another name for a place where the lines cross is an _____ .

6. In the picture, each drawing of a building is a _____ , or one thing that stands for another thing.

Climbing Around

⋛Directions:

Match the word in the left column with its meaning in the right column.

1. mountains

a. a deep valley with steep sides

2. waterfall

b. an area of flat land that is higher than the land around it

3. forest

c. very high hills

4. mesa

d. a sloping, slightly high area near the bottom of a mountain

5. plateau

e. large areas covered with grass; like a prairie

6. canyon

f. stream of water that falls from a high place

7. foothills

g. an area covered with many trees

8. grasslands

h. a hill with steep sides and a wide, flat top

Bonus: Draw the landforms on another sheet of paper. Label the drawings. An example is shown.

Name _____ Date _____

Blow-up!

Directions:
Use the Word Bank to help fill in the blanks.

Word Bank

vent	erupt	ash	cinders
lava	crater	volcano	lake

1. A _____ is a large opening in the earth's surface.

2. This large hole forms when gases and other things _____ .

3. The pieces that are left after something has burned, or _____ , come out of this large hole.

4. Partly burned piece of rock, or _____ , also come out of this large hole.

5. Melted rock, or _____ , flows out of the hole.

6. The _____ is the opening that the melted rock flows through.

7. A _____ is a bowl-shaped opening at the top of the large opening.

8. Sometimes a _____ forms in the bowl-shaped place.

© McGraw-Hill Children's Publishing 0-7424-1933-9 *Theme-Based Vocabulary Builders*

Lots of Wings...and Other Things

⋛Directions:

Use the Word Bank to help unscramble the words. Then write the words.

── Word Bank ──

pine marten	prairie dog	butterfly	golden eagle
brown trout	salamander	lizard	skunk

1. **zdiral** _____

2. **ytlubfert** _____

3. **nowrb torut** _____

4. **epni rntame** _____

5. **unksk** _____

6. **epriira ogd** _____

7. **dnogel agele** _____

8. **rasenlamad** _____

Name _____ Date _____

Using the Land

Directions:

Use the Word Bank to help fill in the blanks.

Word Bank

pueblos	resources	coyote	introduced
shepherds	graze	grassland	predators

1. The first people in this area lived in villages called _____ .

2. These people believed that the land, water, and food, or _____ , are for everyone to use.

3. Later, people from Spain brought, or _____ , sheep into this area.

4. This area has rich _____ .

5. This land is good for cattle and sheep to _____ on.

6. The people who take care of sheep are called _____ .

7. These people keep the sheep safe from _____ , or animals that will eat them.

8. One kind of animal that sometimes eats sheep is a _____ .

Name _____ Date _____

Taking Count

Directions: _____

Use the Word Bank to fill in the blanks.

Word Bank

census	county	community	acres
livestock	shear	traded	land grant

1. Part of the Valles Caldera area was a _____ , or land given to a person by a government.

2. Later, there was a count, or _____ , of people and animals.

3. In this count, a record was made of which _____ someone lived in.

4. The count showed which _____ the person lived in.

5. It also showed how many _____ of land a person owned.

6. Many people owned sheep. Another name that farmers call their animals is _____ .

7. Once a year, the farmers had other people come to cut the wool from their sheep, or _____ them.

8. The farmers then sold or _____ the wool.

© McGraw-Hill Children's Publishing

0-7424-1933-9 *Theme-Based Vocabulary Builders*

Counting Sheep

Directions:

The chart shown is called a *line graph*. This graph shows the number of sheep one person sheared in six days.

A *point* is the place that shows where two pieces of information meet.

A line *segment* is the part of the line that connects two points.

An *intersection* is the place where two points of information meet on a graph.

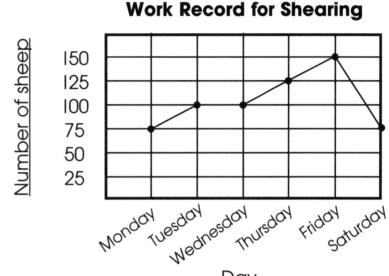

Work Record for Shearing

1. What is one of the labels on the graph? _____

2. What is the other label on the graph? _____

For the next questions, circle the place on the graph about which the questions ask.

3. Where is a *point* on the graph?

4. Where is a *line segment* on the graph?

5. Where is an *intersection* on the graph?

6. Write a different title for the graph. _____

What's My Coat?

Directions: ─────────────────────────────

Does each animal have feathers, fur, scales, or skin? Put a check mark in the correct column.

	feathers	fur	scales	skin
1.				
2.				
3.				
4.				
5.				
6.				

Earth, Water, and Fire

Directions:

Many people around Valles Caldera National Preserve are Native Americans. They make things that their people have made for many years.

Use the Word Bank to help fill in the blanks.

Word Bank

potter	coils	different	clay
pottery	symbols	fired	water

---

1. An artist who makes bowls or jars is called a _____ .

2. The bowls and jars are called _____ .

3. These things are made from _____ , a kind of soil.

4. This soil is mixed with _____ .

5. Then the artists shape the clay into _____ , which look a little like ropes.

6. They add layers of the ropes to make _____ sizes of bowls or jars.

7. When the bowls are shaped, the artist sometimes paints them with _____ , or one thing that stands for another thing.

8. The bowls are then _____ , or heated until they harden.

Climbing and Creeping

Directions:

Use the Word Bank to help unscramble the names of the animals.

── Word Bank ──

rabbit	rattlesnake	bighorn sheep	iguana
tortoise	coyote	scorpion	deer

1. **ered**   _____

2. **tbrabit**   _____

3. **nbrigoh sehep**   _____

4. **trenklesaat**   _____

5. **cyoteo**   _____

6. **erototsi**   _____

7. **opirnsoc**   _____

8. **aignau**   _____

© McGraw-Hill Children's Publishing

0-7424-1933-9 *Theme-Based Vocabulary Builders*

Saving Water

Directions:

Use the Word Bank to help unscramble the names of the plants. Each plant is one that grows in the desert.

Word Bank

juniper	smoke tree	barrel cactus	old man cactus
dwarf sage	greasewood	fluff grass	prickly poppy

1. **klypcir pyopp** _____

2. **afrwd egas** _____

3. **rleabr suatcc** _____

4. **emosk erte** _____

5. **flfuf sgras** _____

6. **erodwogsea** _____

7. **odl anm sctuca** _____

8. **erunipj** _____

Choose two plants from above. Draw what you think they might look like.

Name _____ Date _____

The Water Cycle

⋛Directions: ─────────────────────────

Use the Word Bank to help fill in the blanks. Some words may be used twice.

─── **Word Bank** ───

heat	evaporates	vapor	solid
gas	condenses	liquid	clouds

1. _____ from the sun makes water on the earth change its form.

2. When this happens, it seems that the water disappears, but it _____ .

3. This means that the water changes to a _____.

4. This form of water is called water _____ .

5. When the water _____ rises into the air, it cools.

6. Then the cooled vapor changes back to a _____ .

7. When this happens, we say that the vapor _____ .

8. When the vapor changes, it forms _____ .

9. The _____ form of water is ice.

Science

What Is Matter?

⛭Directions: ───────────────────

Matter is anything that takes up space—air, water, even you! Solve this puzzle to learn more about matter. Use the Word Bank.

─── **Word Bank** ───

change	chemical	gas	liquid
physical	solid	three	

Across

2. There are this many forms of matter: solid, liquid, and gas.

3. Matter can do this.

5. This form of matter has its own shape.

6. This form of matter can be poured.

Down

1. Ice melting is an example of this kind of change.

3. In this kind of change, matter becomes a new substance.

4. This form of matter is very lightweight. It spreads to fill its container.

© McGraw-Hill Children's Publishing

0-7424-1933-9 *Theme-Based Vocabulary Builders*

Sandy Land

Directions:

Match the word in the left column with its meaning in the right column.

1. mountain

   a. a hill with steep sides and a flat top

2. desert

   b. space between hills

3. plateau

   c. a small hole in a hill

4. cave

   d. a low area surrounded by higher land

5. pass

   e. an area of flat land that is higher that the land around it

6. basin

   f. a dry, hot, sandy place

7. mesa

   g. a deep valley with steep sides

8. canyon

   h. a very high hill

Painted Rocks

Directions:

Use the Word Bank to help fill in the blanks.

— Word Bank —

pictographs	petroglyphs	painted
etched	carved	explore

1. The first people to live in the Mojave Desert area _____ pictures on cave walls.

2. These paintings are called _____ .

3. Other pictures were _____ , or cut into rock.

4. Another way to describe this way of making pictures is to say they were _____ .

5. These pictures are called _____ .

6. Today, it is possible to take tours that _____ this area and the cave drawings.

Desert Adventures

⚡Directions: ─────────────────────────

Write a definition for each word. Use a dictionary for any words you do not know.

On another sheet of paper, draw a picture that shows what each word means.

1. canoeing   _____

_____

2. rafting   _____

_____

3. cycling   _____

_____

4. caving   _____

_____

5. hiking   _____

_____

6. climbing   _____

_____

7. photographing   _____

_____

8. rock hounding   _____

_____

Finding Your Place

⸗Directions: ————————————————————————————

Use the Word Bank to help fill in the blanks.

———————— **Word Bank** ————————

| location | point | origin | locate | coordinates |

1. A way to show where things are, or to _____ them, is to use a grid.

2. The _____ is the starting point of a grid. It is usually (0, 0).

3. A _____ is a marked spot.

4. The _____ are a numbered pair that show a place.

5. Another name for a place is _____ .

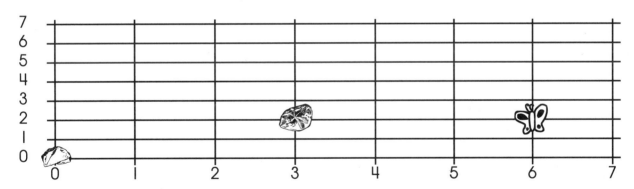

One of the adventures you can have in the Mojave Desert area is to visit fossil beds. Look at the grid to answer the next questions.

6. What thing is at the origin of the grid? _____

7. Where is the fossil? _____

8. What are these points called? _____

© McGraw-Hill Children's Publishing

0-7424-1933-9 *Theme-Based Vocabulary Builders*

Fins, Fur, or Feathers

Directions:

Use the Word Bank to help unscramble the names of the animals.

— Word Bank —

mink	raven	dolphin	skunk
squirrel	porpoise	woodpecker	muskrat

1. **eposirop** _____

2. **nkim** _____

3. **tamkusr** _____

4. **dopwoekcre** _____

5. **kunsk** _____

6. **navre** _____

7. **qrisurle** _____

8. **nhidlop** _____

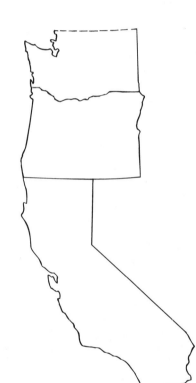

A Zoo for Two

Directions:

Find the two-syllable words to solve the puzzle.

Across

2. horse, catfish, antelope

3. rabbit, ape, hare

4. elephant, otter, pelican

7. hippopotamus, quail, walrus

Down

1. kitten, dog, lamb

3. kangaroo, ant, raccoon

5. hummingbird, eagle, frog

6. rhinoceros, sheep, cougar

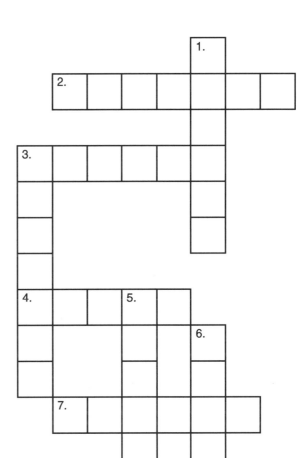

© McGraw-Hill Children's Publishing

0-7424-1933-9 *Theme-Based Vocabulary Builders*

Finding New Places

Directions:

Match the word in the left column to its meaning in the right column.

1. cape   a. an arm or inlet of an ocean

2. explorer   b. a small model of the earth; it is shaped like a sphere

3. harbor   c. land that extends into the sea beyond the rest of the land

4. bay   d. a person who goes into an area to find new things

5. strait   e. a narrow strip of water that connects two other bodies of water

6. basin   f. a dry, hot, sandy place

7. sound   g. a narrow waterway; a way to pass from one body of water to another

8. globe   h. a part of a sea that reaches into land along a shore

Wet and Warm

꞊Directions: ⸺⸺⸺⸺⸺⸺⸺⸺⸺⸺⸺⸺⸺⸺⸺⸺

Match the word in the left column with its meaning in the right column.

1. climate   a. a row of trees that started on nurse logs

2. moisture   b. a place where only some kinds of plants and animals can live

3. rain forest   c. a place saved or set aside for a reason or a use

4. temperature   d. the average, or usual, weather in an area over several years

5. biosphere   e. logs that have seedlings of new trees growing on them

6. reserve   f. small drops of liquid in the air or on the ground

7. nurse logs   g. not very hot or very cold; mild

8. colonnade   h. a woodland that has at least 100 inches of rain each year

By Degrees and Inches

The chart tells you about the weather in two towns near the Olympic National Park.

Quillayute

Month	Average high	Average low	Average rainfall
January	46°	34°	13.8"
June	64°	47°	3.1"

Port Angeles

Month	Average high	Average low	Average rainfall
January	42°	34°	6.1"
June	61°	49°	0"

(continues on page 39)

By Degrees and Inches (cont.)

Directions:

Use the Word Bank to help fill in the blanks.

┌─────────────────── **Word Bank** ───────────────────┐

  alike   converted   centimeters   different

└──┘

1. The temperatures are listed in degrees Fahrenheit. The temperatures could
   be changed, or _____ , to degrees Celsius.

2. The chart makes it easy to see how the temperatures are

   _____ .

3. The chart also makes it easy to see how the temperatures are

   _____ .

4. The amounts of snow or rain are shown in inches. The number of inches
   could be changed to _____ .

Now look at the chart and answer these questions.

5. In January, what was the average temperature in Port Angeles? _____

6. In June, what was the average high temperature in Quillayute? _____

7. What was the average snowfall for Port Angeles in June? _____

8. What was the average rainfall for Quillayute in January? _____

Social studies

Map Your Way

Directions:

Match the word in the left column with its meaning in the right column.

1. map

2. direction

3. key

4. compass

5. distance

6. cardinal directions

7. symbol

8. compass rose

a. the four main points on a compass: north, south, east, and west

b. the amount of space between two points or places

c. a drawing that stands for a real thing

d. a carefully drawn picture of part or all of the earth

e. an instrument that shows direction

f. a drawing on a map that shows directions

g. a list that explains the symbols found on a map

h. the location of a place in relation to the North Pole

A Compass Rose

Directions: ━━━━━━━━━━━━━━━━━━━━━━━━━━

Many very old maps are works of art. The maps that early explorers used often had pictures of dragons or sea monsters to warn of dangers.

In a corner of these maps was a compass rose. Follow the directions to make a compass rose in the top right-hand corner of the map space below. Then make a map of a make-believe land.

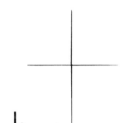

1.

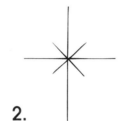

2.

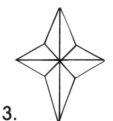

3.

4.

Name _____ Date _____

Plants Big and Small

Directions: ─────────────────────────────
Use the Word Bank and the clues to help unscramble each word.

── Word Bank ──

aspen	blueberry	lichens	fungus
willow	birch	evergreen	moss

1. This tree has bark that peels easily.

   ircbh _____

2. The fruit of this plant can be used for food.

   rybeulebr _____

3. This tree often grows near streams or rivers.

   ilowwl _____

4. These small plants grow on rocks and trees.

   lsinehc _____

5. The name of this tree tells what color it is all year.

   rgenreeve _____

6. These trees have leaves that shake in even a light wind.

   nepsa _____

7. This plant has very small leaves.

   soms _____

8. This plant has no flowers or leaves.

   sugnuf _____

© McGraw-Hill Children's Publishing

0-7424-1933-9 *Theme-Based Vocabulary Builders*

In Air or on Land

≥Directions:

Use the Word Bank to help unscramble the names of the animals.

── Word Bank ──

wolf	grouse	caribou	wolverine
lynx	magpie	brown bear	weasel

1. **ucaorib** _____

2. **folw** _____

3. **saelew** _____

4. **xynl** _____

5. **esrogu** _____

6. **ewonlierv** _____

7. **norbw erab** _____

8. **emiagp** _____

© McGraw-Hill Children's Publishing

0-7424-1933-9 *Theme-Based Vocabulary Builders*

Name _____ Date _____

It's Cold Here!

Directions: ─────────────────────────

Match each word in the left column to its meaning in the right column.

1. tundra

2. arctic

3. terrain

4. meadow

5. refuge

6. taiga

7. frontier

8. permafrost

a. a faraway place where few people live

b. an area where the ground is always frozen

c. a safe place set aside for animals

d. a forest with evergreens and small shrubs

e. an area with no trees and few plants

f. the kind of ground found in a place

g. very cold; an area near the North Pole

h. an area of grassy ground

Name _____ Date _____

A Long Race

Directions:

Use the Word Bank to help fill in the blanks.

── Word Bank ──

relays	remember	tundra	serum	disease
route	mushers	huskies	malamutes	

1. In 1925, children in Nome, Alaska, had a _____ that made them very sick.

2. These children needed a liquid, or _____ , that would help them get well.

3. The best way to get this liquid to Nome was by teams of sled dogs. Some of these dogs are _____ and _____ , kinds of dogs that the native people used.

4. The sled dogs ran in _____ . This means that each team of dogs ran a part of the way to Nome.

5. Every year since 1973, a race called the Iditarod is run to _____ that first run to Nome.

6. The _____ , or the trail that the racers use, goes through mountains, rivers, and _____ .

7. Racers, or _____ , follow lots of rules that make sure they take care of their dogs.

© McGraw-Hill Children's Publishing

0-7424-1933-9 Theme-Based Vocabulary Builders

Keeping Stats

Do you know?

Only one person, Rick Swenson, has won the Iditarod five times.

Only one woman, Susan Butcher, has won the race four times.

Two men, Doug Swingley and Martin Buser, each have won the race four times.

The charts below show the winning times for two racers.

Winning times for Rick Swenson

	days	hours	minutes	seconds
1977	16	16	27	13
1979	15	10	37	47
1981	12	08	45	02
1982	16	04	40	10
1991	12	16	34	39

Winning times for Susan Butcher

	days	hours	minutes	seconds
1986	11	15	06	00
1987	11	02	05	13
1988	11	11	41	40
1990	11	01	53	23

(continues on page 47)

Keeping Stats (cont.)

Directions: _____

Look at the charts on page 46 to answer the questions below.

1. What was Rick Swenson's fastest time? _____

2. What was his second fastest time? _____

3. What was his third fastest time? _____

4. What was his slowest time? _____

5. What was Susan Butcher's fastest time? _____

6. What was her second fastest time? _____

7. What was her third fastest time? _____

8. What was her slowest time? _____

© McGraw-Hill Children's Publishing

0-7424-1933-9 *Theme-Based Vocabulary Builders*

Just in Time

⋛Directions: ───────────────────────────────

Use the Word Bank to help solve the puzzle.

Across

2. February is the only one of these with 28 days.

5. 10 years

7. 60 seconds, or 1 of these

Down

1. a celebration of 100 years

3. 365, or 1 of these

4. 100 years

6. 52 of these, or 1 year

── Word Bank ──

year	centennial	minute	weeks	decade
half hour	century	month	day	

© McGraw-Hill Children's Publishing

0-7424-1933-9 *Theme-Based Vocabulary Builders*

Name _____ Date _____

Baskets from Trees

Directions: ———————————————————

Use the Word Bank to help fill in the blanks.

— Word Bank —

vertical	regrows	sturdy	peel
brace	stitched	dyed	bark

1. The people who live near Denali make baskets of
_____ , or the outside covering, of birch trees.

2. To do this, they make a _____ cut in the tree's
outside covering.

3. Then they _____ the covering from the tree trunk.

4. The outer covering _____ after a while.

5. The baskets are made from this material because it is strong, or
_____ .

6. When the people made baskets, they _____ , the top, or
the rim, with a willow branch.

7. The willow branch is sewn, or _____ , in place with pieces
of roots from spruce trees.

8. Sometimes the roots are _____ to make the baskets
more colorful.

Name _____ Date _____

Three Dimensions

Directions: _____

Use the Word Bank to help fill in the blanks.

─── Word Bank ───

pyramid	cube	hemisphere	rectangular prism
cone	globe	cylinder	sphere

1. This object is shaped like a ball. _____

2. This object is shaped like a ball and is used as a tiny model of the earth. _____

3. This object is shaped like a square box. _____

4. This object is shaped like a pipe. _____

5. This object has a flat base. Its sides look like triangles. _____

6. This object has a flat base and comes to a point. _____

7. This object is shaped like a basket. _____

8. This object looks like a dome. _____

Name _____ Date _____

Simple Shapes

⦂Directions: ─────────────────────────

Look at the drawing below. Then use the Word Bank to find out more about the drawing.

┌──────────────── **Word Bank** ────────────────┐

quilt	fabric strips	textiles	pattern
cloth	design	guide	

└──┘

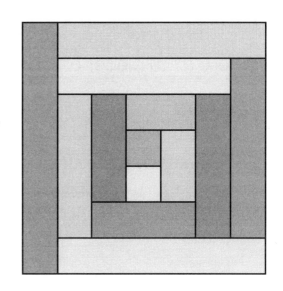

1. This set of shapes is a _____ , or a model. This model is called Log Cabin.

2. People use this model as a _____ .

3. They make many more _____ just like this model.

4. They put these many blocks together to make a _____ , which is a kind of bed covering.

5. This bed covering has two layers of _____ with cotton, wool, or feathers between them.

6. Another word for *cloth* is _____ .

7. Another word for *model* is _____ .

8. How many _____ , or pieces of cloth, are in this model?

Bits 'n Pieces

Directions: _____

Unscramble the letters to make new words. The scrambled words mean the same thing as the words in **bold type.**

1. Women often **used again** fabric from clothing to make quilts.

   clderyce _____

2. Quilts were made of **small pieces** of fabric.

   rpsacs _____

3. These small pieces of fabric were **sewn** together to make a quilt.

   cesithdt _____

4. Another way to say that fabric was **sewn together** is to say that it was was

   _____ .

   eipdce _____

5. The fabric for the back of a quilt had to be one piece. Of all the pieces of a quilt, the back **cost a lot of money.** It was _____ .

   pxeevinse _____

6. Very old quilts are sometimes part of a show at a museum.

   hxitiibe _____

(continues on page 53)

Bits 'n Pieces (cont.)

Directions:

Look again at the pattern. What colors would you use to make a quilt block? Color the pattern. Then draw what the design would look like if you added more blocks to the quilt.

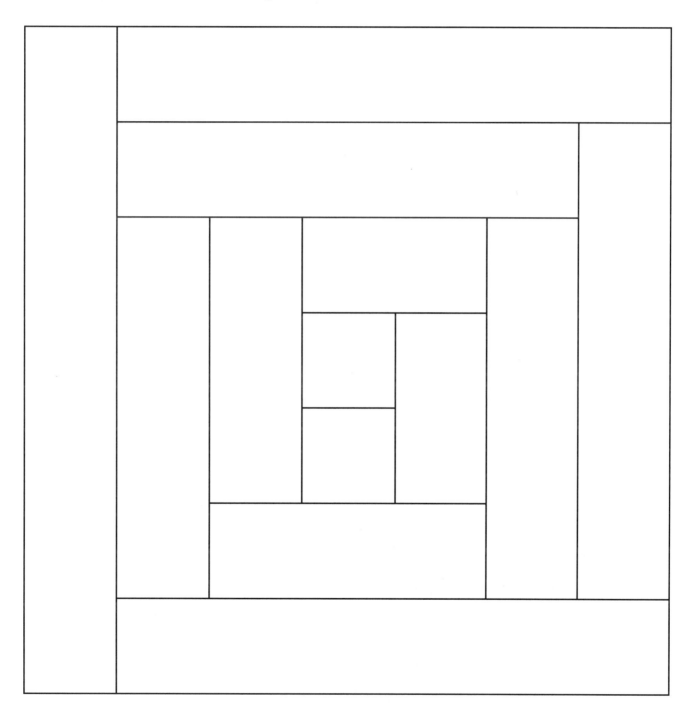

Coloring Cloth

Directions:

Use the Word Bank to help fill in the blanks.

Word Bank

plant	absorbed	shellfish	ore
minerals	indigo	dye	fabric

1. A _____ changes the color of cloth.

2. Dyes can be made from plants, animals, or _____ .

3. A dark blue dye was made from leaves of a _____ .

4. This plant is called _____ . The same name is used for the color.

5. One kind of purple dye came from a _____ .

6. Some yellow dyes come from a mineral, or _____ .

7. In early times, dye was often put into a pot of water. Then the _____ was added.

8. The dye and fabric were boiled until the fabric _____ the dye.

Name _____ Date _____

Changing Colors

⭢Directions:

Use the Word Bank to help fill in the blanks.

— Word Bank —

primary	violet	lightens	green
darkens	blue	secondary	mixing

1. Red, blue, and yellow are the only colors that cannot be made by
   _____ two other colors.

2. They are called _____ colors.

3. Mixing red and yellow makes orange. Orange is a _____ color.

4. Yellow and blue mixed together make _____ . Green is a
   _____ color.

5. The third _____ color is purple. It is made by mixing red and
   _____ .

6. Another name for *purple* is _____ .

7. Mixing black with a color _____ the color.

8. Mixing white with a color _____ the color.

© McGraw-Hill Children's Publishing

0-7424-1933-9 *Theme-Based Vocabulary Builders*

Name _____ Date _____

Line and Color

⩾Directions: _____

Use the Word Bank to help fill in the blanks.

── Word Bank ──

layers	canvas	oil	lines
palette	primary	horizontal	vertical

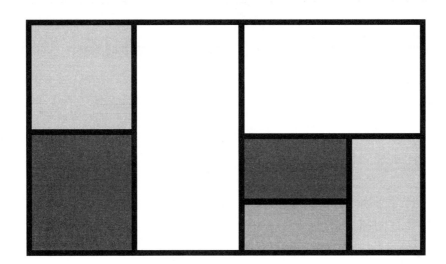

1. Piet Mondrian (1872–1944) used only _____ and colors in his paintings.

2. Some of the lines are _____ , which means they go up and down.

3. Other lines go from side to side, or are _____ .

4. He liked to use _____ paint.

5. Artists who want to mix paints use a _____ .

6. Mondrian most often used _____ colors instead of mixing paints.

7. He painted on _____ .

8. He liked to use _____ of paint.

Name _____ Date _____

Brightness from the Sun

Directions:

Use the Word Bank to help fill in the blanks.

— Word Bank —

energy	bands	lamps	solar
wave	rainbow	sun	flashlights

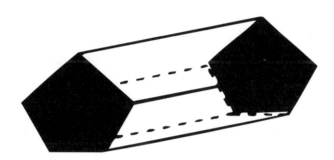

1. Light is brightness that comes from the _____ .

2. This brightness can come from other sources, like _____ and _____ .

3. Another name for this brightness is _____ .

4. A word that means "coming from the sun" is _____ .

5. The color of a light _____ depends on the amount of energy that it carries.

6. A prism breaks light into _____ of color.

7. These bands of color can be seen in a _____ .

Clear or Colored

Directions: ————————————————————

Use the Word Bank to fill in the blanks.

———— Word Bank ————

metals	discovered	furnace	eyeglasses
minerals	melting	windows	potters

1. Glass is made by _____ sand, soda, and lime at very high temperatures.

2. The sand, soda, and lime are heated in a _____ .

3. To make some colors of glass, _____ like gold or silver are added.

4. To make other colors of glass, _____ are added.

5. The way to make glass was found, or _____ , in what is now Syria and Iraq.

6. The people who found the way to make glass were _____ .

7. Then and today, glass is used for bowls and _____ .

8. Today, glass is also used for mirrors and _____ .

Name _____   Date _____

Colored Windows

Directions:
Use the Word Bank to help fill in the blanks.

Word Bank

stained	cathedrals	mosaic
stories	symbols	pieces

---

1. Hundreds of years ago, people in Europe built very large churches called

   _____ .

2. In these churches, artists made windows of

   colored, or _____ , glass.

3. Some designs in the windows told

   _____ .

4. Other designs were _____ ,
   or things that stand for or mean another
   thing.

5. These windows often had lots of small
   _____ of colored
   glass in them.

6. The small pieces of glass made the
   windows look like a _____ .

Using Glass

≡Directions: ————————————————————————

Use the Word Bank to help fill in the blanks.

——— Word Bank ———

pastel	windows	cathedrals
style	public	recall

1. For many years after the _____ were built, people did not use much stained glass.

2. By the 1850s, they started to _____ how to make and use stained glass.

3. About a hundred years ago, people began to use colored glass in the _____ of their homes.

4. This glass had softer, more _____ colors than the cathedral glass did.

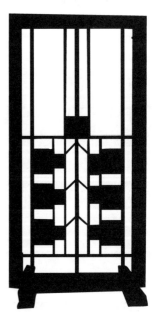

5. A man who used clear and colored glass in _____ buildings was Frank Lloyd Wright (1869–1959).

6. His designs were called Prairie _____ .

Name _____ Date _____

Lines and Corners

Directions: ─────────────────────────
Use the Word Bank to fill in the blanks.

┌──────────────── **Word Bank** ────────────────┐

polygon	dimensions	plane	parallel
three	next	vertical	measure

└──┘

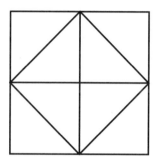

The pattern shown is similar to one that an artist might use to make a stained-glass window.

1. The glass is a flat surface, or a _____ .

2. The pattern, or design, is a _____ .

3. It has horizontal and _____ lines in it.

4. The pattern also has _____ lines in it.

5. The artist plans which colors will be _____ to each other in the design.

6. Before cutting the pieces of glass, the artist will _____ the lines and corners.

7. This pattern has two _____ .

8. Some designs are in _____ dimensions.

© McGraw-Hill Children's Publishing

0-7424-1933-9 *Theme-Based Vocabulary Builders*

Figuring It Out

Directions: _____

Use the Word Bank and clues to help solve the puzzle.

Across

2. In 6 + 7 = 13, the 6 and the 7 are these.

4. 8 + 7 = 15 is this.

6. a part of a whole

Down

1. to put numbers together, as 7 + 9 = 16

3. guessing how many there are

5. In 16 ÷ 8 = 2, 2 is called this.

6. In 5 x 6 = 30, the 5 or 6 is called this.

7. the outside surface of something

Word Bank

add	equation	perimeter	addends	sum
quotient	fraction	multiply	area	subtract
factor	estimating	times		

© McGraw-Hill Children's Publishing

0-7424-1933-9 *Theme-Based Vocabulary Builders*

Making a Design

Directions: ──────────────────────────

Use the pattern shown to make a stained-glass design.

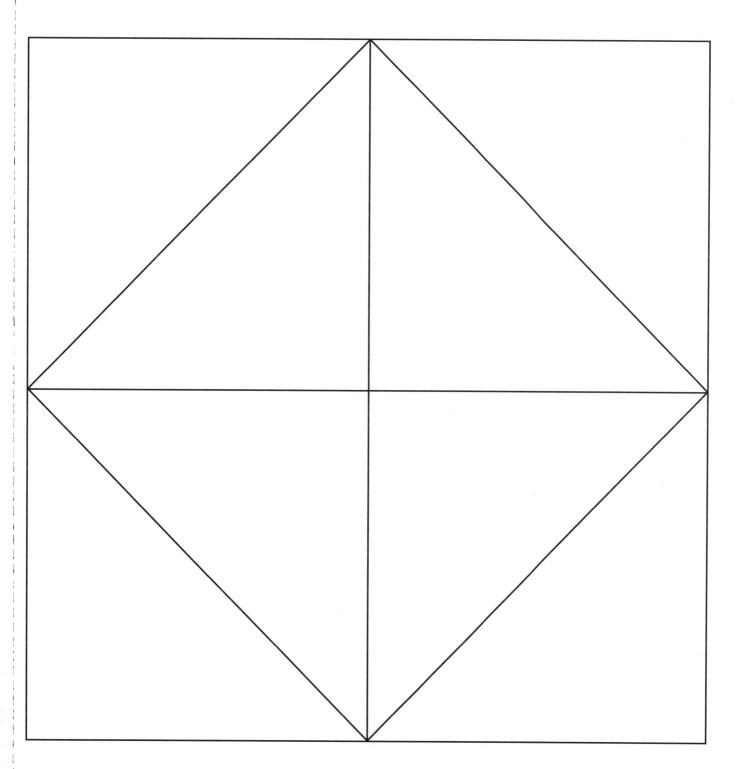

In the Jungle

Directions: _____

Use the Word Bank to help unscramble the name of each animal.

Word Bank

cougars	iguanas	monkeys	tapirs	crocodiles
parrots	jaguars	opossums	alligators	toucans

1. **aujsgar** _____

2. **ncustoa** _____

3. **artisp** _____

4. **patorsr** _____

5. **arusgoc** _____

6. **lrsiloagta** _____

7. **ymesnok** _____

8. **smosupos** _____

9. **smosupos** _____

10. **decrilcoso** _____

© McGraw-Hill Children's Publishing

0-7424-1933-9 *Theme-Based Vocabulary Builders*

Highs and Lows

Directions:

Match the word in the left column with its meaning in the right column.

1. desert

2. plateau

3. jungle

4. volcano

5. grassland

6. swamp

7. lagoon

8. scrubland

a. an area that gets lots of rain; covered with trees and plants

b. an area of muddy land that is often filled with water

c. a flat area that is higher than the land around it

d. a shallow body of water along a shore

e. a hole in the earth that lava, dust, and ash come from

f. land covered with very small shrubs or trees

g. a very dry area

h. an area like a prairie; covered with grass

Name _____ Date _____

Steps to the Sky

Directions:

Use the Word Bank to help fill in the blanks. Some words may be used twice.

Word Bank

concept	stairways	altogether	system
canals	calendar	symbols	

1. The Mayans lived in the western part of Mexico. They had a _____ of numbers.

2. It used three _____ .

3. The Mayans had pyramids with four _____ , each with 91 steps.

4. The pyramids have 365 steps _____ , or one for each day of the year.

5. The Mayans had a _____ , or idea, of zero.

6. Their _____ had 365 days in it.

7. Their religious leaders studied the stars and planets. This is called _____ .

8. The Aztecs lived near what is now Mexico City. They built bridges and _____ to make an island-city.

9. They had a _____ with 360 days in it.

© McGraw-Hill Children's Publishing

0-7424-1933-9 *Theme-Based Vocabulary Builders*

What a Ride!

Directions:

Unscramble the words to make the names of the planets found in the maze. Write the answers on the lines.

The Mayans studied stars and planets, but they could not take the ride that you will take. To find your way through the maze, start at the comet and draw a line to the answer for number 1. Keep going until you reach the home satellite.

1. **sram** _____

2. **ntsaur** _____

3. **nusrau** _____

4. **svneu** _____

5. **htrae**

6. **putjire** _____

7. **cryreum** _____

8. **ptennue** _____

9. **optlu** _____

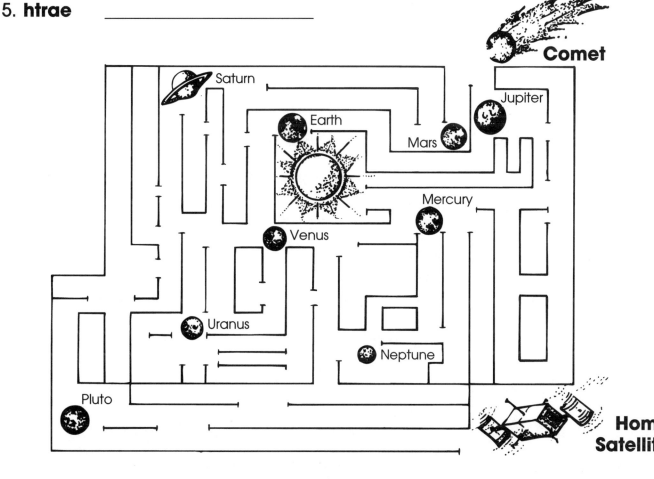

Painting on Walls

Directions: _____

Use the Word Bank to help fill in the blanks.

— Word Bank —

display	industry	national	pride
murals	workers	frescos	history

A famous Mexican
artist was Diego
Rivera (1886–1954).

1. Rivera was famous for his _____ , which he painted on walls.

2. He liked to paint _____ and their work.

3. One of his best-known paintings was done in Detroit, Michigan. This painting
   was about science and _____ .

4. In Mexico, Rivera did paintings called _____ .

5. These paintings were on the wall of _____ buildings.

6. The paintings tell stories about the _____ of Mexico.

7. He wanted Mexicans to have _____ in their country.

8. If you go to Mexico City today, you can see some of his murals on

   _____ .

Fur and Feathers

⌇Directions: ─────────────────────────────────

Use the Word Bank to help unscramble the names of the animals.

── Word Bank ──

beaver	Canada goose	raccoon	otter	walrus
lynx	bighorn sheep	moose	pheasant	gopher

1. **xyln** _____

2. **ocanocr** _____

3. **natepash** _____

4. **asrluw** _____

5. **troet** _____

6. **rgohibn peseh** _____

7. **arebev** _____

8. **anacda sogoe** _____

9. **pehrog** _____

10. **somoe** _____

Name _____ Date _____

High and Low

Directions:

Match each word in the left column with its meaning in the right column.

1. tundra   a. areas of low, flat lands

2. strait   b. a long, narrow body of water
                      between high slopes

3. glacier   c. large, flat areas with no trees

4. peninsula   d. a line that separates one
                      country or state from another

5. lowlands   e. a cold area that has no trees and few plants

6. border   f. a very large area of land

7. plains   g. a line of mountains

8. continent   h. a narrow body of water that connects two larger
                      bodies of water

9. range   i. a very large piece of ice that moves slowly

10. fjord   j. a piece of land with water on three sides of it

© McGraw-Hill Children's Publishing   0-7424-1933-9 *Theme-Based Vocabulary Builders*

Name _____ Date _____

What Do You Do?

Directions:

Some people in Canada, especially the Inuit and other native people, use old ways to do work. Use a dictionary for any words you do not know. Write a description of each type of work. On a separate piece of paper, draw a picture of what each word means.

1. fishing _____

2. hunting _____

3. trapping _____

4. trading _____

5. farming _____

6. mining _____

© McGraw-Hill Children's Publishing

0-7424-1933-9 *Theme-Based Vocabulary Builders*

Name _____   Date _____

Natural Beauty

Directions: _____

Use the Word Bank to help fill in the blanks.

— Word Bank —

drawings	natural	bones	dollmakers
carve	antlers	weave	paint

1. Inuit artists look at the _____ world, or the things around them.

2. Some of them _____ animals or birds from stone.

3. Some of them use _____ from whales.

4. Others use _____ from animals.

5. Some women artists _____ , or make cloth.

6. _____ make figures that look like mothers carrying children.

7. Pencils and paper are used to make _____ .

8. Other artists _____ pictures of how life was in the past.

Name _____ Date _____

Where Is It?

⫶Directions: ────────────────────────

Use the Word Bank and the picture to help fill in the blanks.

─── **Word Bank** ───

directions	north	east	west
south	cardinal	compass rose	map

1. A _____ is a picture that shows a place.

2. A map shows which _____ things are.

3. There are four main, or _____ , directions.

4. The _____ tells where the directions are on a map.

5. On a map the top, or up, is always _____ .

6. On this map, _____ is to the left.

7. To the right is _____ .

8. Down, or the bottom of this map, is _____ .

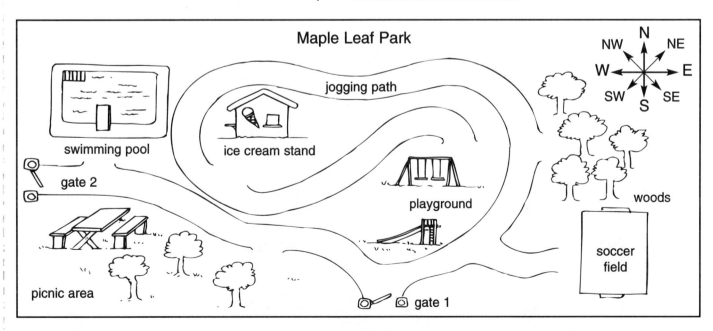

Maple Leaf Park

Claws 'n Paws

≡Directions:

Use the Word Bank to unscramble the name of each animal.

Word Bank

dugong	wallaby	koala	kangaroo	platypus
dingo	emu	crocodile	wombat	penguin

1. **akola** _____

2. **odgni** _____

3. **mabowt** _____

4. **ecrilocdo** _____

5. **gongud** _____

6. **okragano** _____

7. **lbawyla** _____

8. **ume** _____

9. **negipun** _____

10. **spualytp** _____

© McGraw-Hill Children's Publishing

0-7424-1933-9 *Theme-Based Vocabulary Builders*

Say "G'day"

⫷Directions: ─────────────────────────────────

Use the Word Bank to help fill in the blanks.

── Word Bank ──

interior	coral	desert	island	plateaus
bush	graze	continent	outback	

1. Australia is the largest _____ in the world.

2. It is also the smallest _____ .

3. The Australians call the countryside the _____ .

4. The inside, or _____ , of the country is called the

   _____ .

5. Cows and sheep _____ in this area.

6. Part of Australia is a _____ .

7. Other parts of Australia are low _____ .

8. The Great Barrier Reef is a _____ reef.

© McGraw-Hill Children's Publishing 0-7424-1933-9 *Theme-Based Vocabulary Builders*

Name _____ Date _____

Making Art

⸖Directions:

The native people in Australia, the Aborigines, have arts that parents pass on to children.

Use the Word Bank to help fill in the blanks. Use a dictionary to find the meaning of any words you do not know.

— Word Bank —

bark painting	didjeridoo	stone etchings	pipes
storytelling	boomerang	woven baskets	wood carvings

1. **entso csegtinh**   _____

2. **tgsniotrlyle**   _____

3. **psipe**   _____

4. **abkr gpniiatn**   _____

5. **dowo sagcirnv**   _____

6. **ongboaerm**   _____

7. **evnow tsabeks**   _____

8. **oddjdoirei**   _____

© McGraw-Hill Children's Publishing

0-7424-1933-9 *Theme-Based Vocabulary Builders*

Measure It Up

Directions:

Look at the pattern. Use the Word Bank to help fill in the blanks.

Word Bank

tall	measurement	straight	metric
wide	round	centimeters	converted

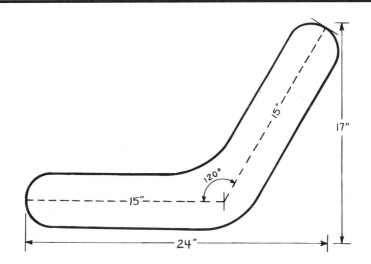

1. The _____ on the right side of the pattern is in inches.

2. The number tells how _____ the boomerang is.

3. The number at the bottom of the pattern tells how _____ the boomerang is.

4. The sides of the boomerang are _____ lines.

5. The ends of the boomerang are _____ .

6. The numbers can be changed, or _____ , to a different way of measurement.

7. That way of measurement is called the _____ system. It is used in Australia.

8. In Australia, the numbers would be in _____ .

For Good Measure

Directions: _____

Use the Word Bank and the clues to help solve the puzzle.

Across

2. degrees in the metric system

6. There are 16 in 1 pound.

7. There are 12 in 1 foot.

8. There are 3 feet in 1 of these.

Down

1. metric liquid measurement

3. There are 12 inches in 1 of these.

4. There are 100 of them in 1 meter.

5. There are 2 of these in 1 quart.

Word Bank

inches	pints	ounces	foot
yard	liters	centimeters	kilograms
degrees	grams	meter	ton
quarts	pounds	Celsius	

© McGraw-Hill Children's Publishing

0-7424-1933-9 *Theme-Based Vocabulary Builders*

Science

Stripes 'n Things

Directions:
Use the Word Bank to help unscramble the names of the animals.

Word Bank

elephant	deer	gazelle	tiger	sloth bear
monkey	mongoose	parrot	cobra	cattle

1. **rede** _____

2. **gitre** _____

3. **nekyom** _____

4. **tarpor** _____

5. **acorb** _____

6. **etalct** _____

7. **emsogosno** _____

8. **tolsh erab** _____

9. **eglazel** _____

10. **epalhent** _____

© McGraw-Hill Children's Publishing

0-7424-1933-9 *Theme-Based Vocabulary Builders*

Land of Contrasts

Directions: ——————————————————————

Match the word in the left column with its meaning in the right column.

1. climate
2. boundary
3. plain
4. peninsula
5. tributary
6. subcontinent
7. hemisphere
8. equator

a. half of a sphere; a half of the earth

b. a part of a continent

c. an imaginary line around the center of the earth

d. a stream that flows into a larger stream or river

e. a line that separates one country or state from another

f. the usual weather conditions in an area over time

g. a flat or slightly rolling area

h. land that has water on three sides

Name _____ Date _____

Seeds and Leaves

⋛Directions: ───────────────

In India, each cook makes a blend of spices for cooking. Match the word in the left column with its meaning in the right column. The words will tell you about some of the spices used in India.

1. parsley   a. a plant that is related to onions

2. mustard   b. the bark of a tree, used as a spice

3. garlic   c. the dried flower bud of a plant

4. cinnamon   d. the seeds of a plant used to season and to make a condiment

5. cloves   e. a leafy plant that is a member of the carrot family

6. ginger   f. the root of a plant

© McGraw-Hill Children's Publishing

0-7424-1933-9 *Theme-Based Vocabulary Builders*

Name _____ Date _____

At the Movies

☰ Directions:

Use the Word Bank to fill in the blanks.

— Word Bank —

sitar	movies	melody	written
invents	scale	important	theme

1. In India, people like to go to _____ .

2. An _____ part of a movie is the music.

3. Indian music has only a _____ , or a tune.

4. It uses a _____ of seven notes.

5. Each of these groups of notes has a _____ , such as a season.

6. Indian music is not _____ down.

7. Instead, each musician makes it up, or _____ it, as he or she plays.

8. A _____ is an instrument that is popular in India.

© McGraw-Hill Children's Publishing

0-7424-1933-9 *Theme-Based Vocabulary Builders*

It's the Same

Directions:

Use the Word Bank and the pictures to help fill in the blanks. Some words may be used twice.

Word Bank

half	same	flip	turn
grid	pattern	symmetry	

1. If you _____ the picture, it will look like this.

2. If you _____ the picture, it will look like this.

3. This picture is a _____ of the Taj Mahal, a famous building in India.

4. This picture is drawn on a _____ .

5. One _____ of the building is shown.

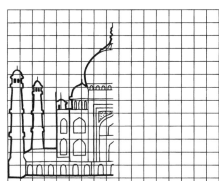

6. You could draw the other _____ of the building.

7. It would be the _____ as the first part.

8. When the two halves of something are the same, this is called _____ .

© McGraw-Hill Children's Publishing

0-7424-1933-9 *Theme-Based Vocabulary Builders*

Brrrr!

Directions:

Match each winter weather word to the definition.

1. blizzard   a. a low temperature; not warm

2. wind   b. to become solid by lack of heat

3. freeze   c. water that is solid, not liquid

4. ice   d. air that moves and blows around

5. cold   e. a very long storm with wind and heavy snow

6. frost   f. pellets of ice

7. sleet   g. a pile of something that has been blown by the wind

8. drift   h. soft, white flakes

9. snow   i. rain that is partly frozen

10. hail   j. a thin layer of ice crystals

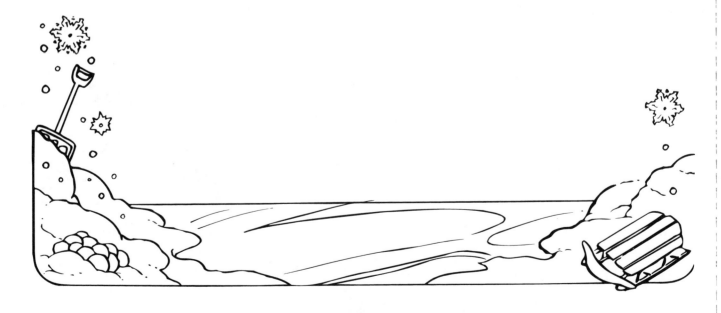

Racing Along

⊰Directions:

Use the Word Bank to help you unscramble the words. Each word is the name of a sport in the Winter Olympics.

── Word Bank ──

figure skating	snowboarding	luge	skiing
speed skating	bobsledding	hockey	

1. **gbnoibdsdle** _____

2. **gskini** _____

3. **egufir gskinta** _____

4. **elgu** _____

5. **yheock** _____

6. **gsnonidwobar** _____

7. **edspe atikgns** _____

Name _____ Date _____

Near or Far

⇒Directions: ────────────────────────────

Use the Word Bank to help fill in the blanks. Some words may be used twice.

──────── Word Bank ────────

tilts	orbits	hemisphere
summer	winter	

1. The earth moves around, or _____ the sun.

2. The earth also _____ , or is at an angle to the sun.

3. The northern half, or _____ , of the earth is farther away from the sun in the winter.

4. In the United States, the earth get less heat and light from the sun in _____ than in summer.

5. The southern _____ of the earth receives more light and heat during those months.

6. When it is winter in the United States, it is _____ in the southern half of the earth.

Chinese New Year

Directions: ─────────────────────────

Match the word in the left column to its definition in the right column. Each word describes something that is part of the Chinese New Year.

1. unity

    a. a plant with thin, flexible stems that are used to make things

2. lantern

    b. cloth made from a shiny fiber made by worms

3. feast

    c. seeds that are cooked and eaten

4. firecracker

    d. a paper covering for a light

5. rice

    e. a large, special meal

6. silk

    f. an imaginary animal that looks like a big lizard

7. dragon

    g. something set off to make noise

8. bamboo

    h. agreeing; forming a whole

© McGraw-Hill Children's Publishing

0-7424-1933-9 *Theme-Based Vocabulary Builders*

Social studies

Kwanzaa

Directions:

Use the Word Bank to help fill in the blanks.

Word Bank

| history | community | candles | unity |
| culture | celebrate | feast | goals |

1. Kwanzaa is a winter holiday. Many African American people
   _____ it as a special time.

2. Families use this time to think about African _____ .

3. Kwanzaa reminds African Americans that they are a _____
   with common interests.

4. The _____ of Africa is honored in Kwanzaa.

5. Part of the Kwanzaa tradition is lighting _____ for seven days.

6. During Kwanzaa, families think about seven _____ , one for
   each day.

7. An important part of Kwanzaa is
   _____ .

8. Another important part of Kwanzaa is a large
   family meal, or _____ .

Lining Things Up

Directions: ─────────────────────────────

Use the Word Bank to help fill in the blanks.

───── Word Bank ─────

| labels | line | point | segment | title | snow |

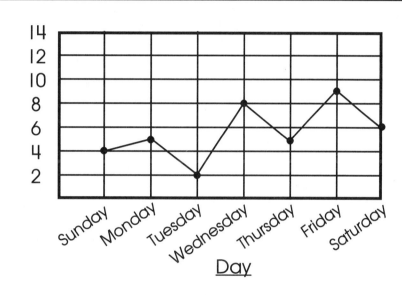

1. This kind of graph is called a _____ graph.

2. The place where two parts of information meet on a graph is called a

   _____ .

3. The _____ are at the side and bottom of a graph.

4. The line between two parts of information is called a line

   _____ .

5. The _____ is the name of the graph.

6. This graph measures how much _____ fell in one week.

7. What are the labels on this graph? _____

8. Write a title for the graph. _____

Rain or Shine

≡**Directions:** ─────────────────────────────

Match each word in the left column with its meaning in the right column.

1. fog

    a. small drops of water on things that are close to the ground

2. cloud

    b. a cloud that is close to the ground

3. rain

    c. weather with few clouds, no rain, and comfortable temperatures

4. sunny

    d. a group of small drops of water hanging in the air

5. hail

    e. drops of water that fall to the earth

6. drizzle

    f. small pieces of ice

7. dew

    g. weather with almost no clouds

8. fair

    h. very small drops of water

Flowery Words

Directions:

Use the Word Bank to solve the riddles.

--- Word Bank ---

stem	flower	coat	root	water
sun	leaf	chlorophyll	carbon dioxide	

1. I protect you and seeds from bad weather. _____

2. I hold hair in your head and a plant in the ground. _____

3. A plant cannot live without me, but you need protection from me.

   _____

4. A camel and a cactus can store me for a long time. _____

5. I'm a gas that is helpful to plants, but I can't be bought at a gas station.

   _____

6. Many plants show my colors proudly. _____

7. When I grow, the plant gets taller. _____

8. I may change colors, but I'm not a
   chameleon. _____

9. I'm always green, but not with envy.

   _____

Counting Flowers

⋛Directions: ───────────────────────────

A gardener might want to count how many of each kind of flower she plants in a day. Use the Word Bank to help fill in the blanks.

─────── Word Bank ───────

| symbol | key | record | pictograph |

1. One way she can count is to _____, or keep track of, her information.

2. The graph shown is one way to keep track of information. This kind of graph is called a _____ .

3. The _____ is the picture that shows the amount of information.

4. The _____ is the box that shows the value of each picture.

Look at the graph to answer the next questions.

Flower	
Lily	✿ ✿ ✿
Rose	✿ ✿ ✿ ✿ ✿ (✿) -------
Violet	✿

Key   (1 ✿ = 5 plants) - - - - - - - - -

5. On this graph, what is the key? Write the word by the dotted line.

6. On this graph, what is the symbol? Write the word by the dotted line.

7. Write a title for the table. _____

8. What three kinds of flowers did this gardener plant? Use a dictionary to look up any words you do not know. _____

Cinco de Mayo

≥Directions: ————————————————————————

On May 5, 1862, Mexican soldiers won a fight, or *battle,* with a French army. Cinco de Mayo (the fifth of May) celebrates this day.

Many Spanish words are part of the English language. Some Spanish words have changed in spelling. Others are the same in Spanish and in English. Match each word in the left column with the words in the right column that mean the same.

1. piñata

2. cafeteria

3. mariachi

4. mercado

5. fiesta

6. chili

7. sombrero

8. vanilla

9. poncho

10. tortilla

a. celebration or festival

b. a flavoring made from the seeds of an orchid

c. a pottery or cardboard form filled with candies or small gifts

d. a thick sauce of beans and hot peppers

e. a Mexican street band

f. a market, or a place where people buy and sell things

g. a round, flat bread baked on a grill

h. a place to buy food; a coffee shop (in Spanish)

i. a hat with a wide brim

j. a body covering with a hole in the center for a person's head

© McGraw-Hill Children's Publishing

0-7424-1933-9 *Theme-Based Vocabulary Builders*

Name _____ Date _____

Spinning Around

Directions:

Use the Word Bank to help fill in the blanks. Some words may be used twice.
You may need to use a dictionary.

— Word Bank —

equinox	orbits	pole	spring
equator	autumn	axis	

1. Earth moves around, or _____ the sun.

2. The earth rotates on an _____ , or an
   imaginary straight line runs through its center.

3. The earth has an imaginary line, or _____ around its middle.

4. This line is the same distance from the north _____ and the
   south _____ .

5. Two times each year, the sun crosses the _____ .

6. For those two times, day and night are the same length everywhere.
   This time is called an _____ .

7. One of those times is the first day of _____ .

8. The other time is the first day of _____ .

© McGraw-Hill Children's Publishing

0-7424-1933-9 *Theme-Based Vocabulary Builders*

Fiesta!

Directions: ——————————————————

Use the Word Bank to fill in the blanks. The words will tell you more about
Cinco de Mayo.

—————————————— **Word Bank** ——————————————

ballad	fireworks	nature	marching
perform	freedom	dances	piñata

1. Cinco de Mayo celebrates _____ .

2. A parade with _____ bands is part of the day.

3. People often sing a _____ , or song, called "DeColores."

4. "DeColores" is about the colors in _____ , or the world
   around us.

5. Some musicians play, or _____ , mariachi music.

6. Other people do folk _____ that have been taught by
   parents to their children.

7. In the evening there is a _____ for the children.

8. There are _____ for everyone to watch.

Name _____ Date _____

Playing Games

≥Directions:

Use the Word Bank. Unscramble the names of these sports that are
a part of the Olympics.

── Word Bank ──

cycling	boxing	baseball	sailing	softball
diving	canoeing	tennis	volleyball	basketball

1. **stnien** _____

2. **ygnccli** _____

3. **sfblaot** _____

4. **gdiinv** _____

5. **lbalakset** _____

6. **sganiil** _____

7. **lbaalbse** _____

8. **loalylblve** _____

9. **ganecion** _____

10. **nxoibg** _____

Jesse Owens

Bonus: Jesse Owens set five world records at the 1936 Olympics in Berlin.
Use a dictionary or an encyclopedia to find out more about him.

Name _____ Date _____

Mostly Sunny

Directions:

Match the weather word in the left column with its meaning in the right column.

1. sunny

a. the sound that happens when lightning heats the air and makes it expand

2. fog

b. how warm or cold the air is

3. lightning

c. fog and bits of pollution in the air

4. temperature

d. a quick, short increase in how fast the wind blows

5. smog

e. weather with a cloudless sky

6. humidity

f. flashes of light that we see when electricity passes from cloud to cloud

7. thunder

g. a cloud that is close to the ground

8. gust

h. the amount of water vapor in the air

© McGraw-Hill Children's Publishing

0-7424-1933-9 *Theme-Based Vocabulary Builders*

Keeping Track

Directions:

Use the Word Bank to help fill in the blanks.

Word Bank

bar   vertical   bar graph

People who coach summer sports want to know how many children play each sport. One way for them to do this is shown below.

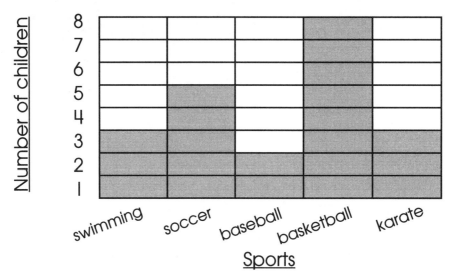

1. This graph is a _____ graph, or a graph with columns or

   rows that go from bottom to top.

2. Each shaded part of the graph is called a _____ .

3. The whole graph is called a _____ .

Look at the graph to answer the following questions.

4. What is one of the labels on the graph? _____

5. Which bar shows the most children playing a sport? _____

6. What is the other label? _____

7. Which bar shows the sport with the least number of children playing?

   _____

8. Write a title for the graph. _____

The Fourth of July

Directions:

Use the Word Bank to help fill in the blanks.

Word Bank

civil rights	freedom	capital	elections	equal
protest	sit-ins	picnic	boycotted	

1. The Fourth of July celebrates _____ .

2. Being free means being treated in an _____ way.

3. Many African Americans were not treated like other people. Sometimes they could not vote in _____ .

4. In the summer of 1963, many African Americans were part of the March on Washington, the _____ of the United States.

5. This march was a _____ about the way that African Americans were treated.

6. In the southern part of the country, people had _____ because they were sometimes not served in restaurants.

7. In some cities, people _____ , or did not use, the buses. This was because African Americans could sit only in the back of the buses.

8. In the summer of 1964, a _____ law gave African Americans the right to vote. This law also let them go to the places they wanted to go.

9. People show they are happy to be free in many ways. One way is to have a _____ .

A Fall Feast

Directions:

Use the Word Bank to help unscramble the words.

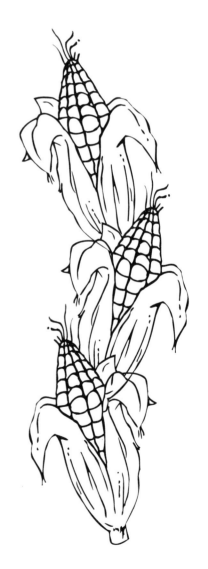

— Word Bank —

squash	corn	eel	beans
geese	oysters	ducks	pumpkin
cranberries	turkeys	mushrooms	gooseberries

1. **sbane** _____

2. **yutksre** _____

3. **shaqus** _____

4. **scudk** _____

5. **orcn** _____

6. **ostyres** _____

7. **ele** _____

8. **nipkump** _____

9. **segee** _____

10. **sebrcarnir** _____

11. **osrmuohms** _____

12. **rbeserogoessi** _____

Whole or Part

Directions:

Draw a line from the word in the left column to a word or words in the right column that mean the same.

1. fraction   a. two times

2. double   b. three times

3. triple   c. complete

4. whole   d. part of a whole

Look at the pictures to find the correct answer.

5. Color the set of figures that shows parts of a whole.

a. 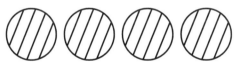   b.

6. Color the circle that shows a circle divided in half.

a.    b.

© McGraw-Hill Children's Publishing

0-7424-1933-9 *Theme-Based Vocabulary Builders*

Going in a Circle

≋**Directions:** ─────────────────────────

Use the Word Bank to help fill in the blanks.

─── **Word Bank** ───

fruit	order	adult	seed
flowers	cycle	seedling	

1. Plants with flowers have a life _____ , or things that happen over and over.

2. The same things happen in the same _____ .

3. A plant starts from a _____ , or a small, closed part.

4. From the small closed part comes a _____ , or a small, new plant.

5. The new, small plant becomes an _____ , or a fully grown plant.

6. The fully grown plant has _____ or _____ , the parts of the plant that makes more small, closed parts.

© McGraw-Hill Children's Publishing

0-7424-1933-9 *Theme-Based Vocabulary Builders*

Giving Thanks

Directions:

Use the Word Bank to help fill in the blanks. Some words may be used more than once.

Word Bank

worship	hardships	Pilgrims	*Mayflower*
Thanksgiving	Compact	grateful	

1. The first English people to live in what is now Massachusetts were called _____ .

2. They left England because they could not _____ as they wanted.

3. They sailed on a ship called the _____ .

4. They agreed on a way to live in the new land they had found. This agreement was called the Mayflower _____ .

5. The _____ landed in the winter of 1620.

6. That first winter was full of _____ .

7. In the spring, the Pilgrims had a feast to show that they were _____ for living through the winter.

8. Later, people called that feast _____ and celebrated it in November.

At the Table

Directions: _____

Use the Word Bank to fill in the blanks.

— Word Bank —

real	huge	style
family	lines	painted

1. In 1943, Norman Rockwell (1894–1978) _____ a picture called "Freedom from Want."

2. The picture shows a _____ of children, parents, and grandparents.

3. The family is ready to eat a _____ Thanksgiving feast.

4. Rockwell made things in his painting look _____ .

5. His way, or _____ , of painting is different from the way some artists paint.

6. Some artists use only _____ , shapes, and colors in their paintings.

In the Fields

⋛Directions: ─────────────────────────────────

Use the Word Bank. Unscramble the words that tell what crops and foods people in Greece grew many hundreds of years ago.

── Word Bank ──

barley	figs	hay	wheat
olives	beans	grapes	lentils

1. **seban** _____

2. **rsapeg** _____

3. **violes** _____

4. **tehwa** _____

5. **gisf** _____

6. **ybalre** _____

7. **ahy** _____

8. **lsenilt** _____

The First Olympics

⋛Directions:

The first Olympic Games were held in Greece many hundreds of years ago.

Each word below names a sport that the Greeks played. Write a definition for each. Use your dictionary to find the meaning of any words you do not know.

Then draw a picture to show what the word means.

1. boxing _____

   _____

2. wrestling _____

   _____

3. horse racing _____

   _____

4. running _____

   _____

5. chariot racing _____

   _____

© McGraw-Hill Children's Publishing
0-7424-1933-9 *Theme-Based Vocabulary Builders*

In Good Health

⋛Directions: ─────────────────────────

Match the word in the left column with its meaning in the right column.

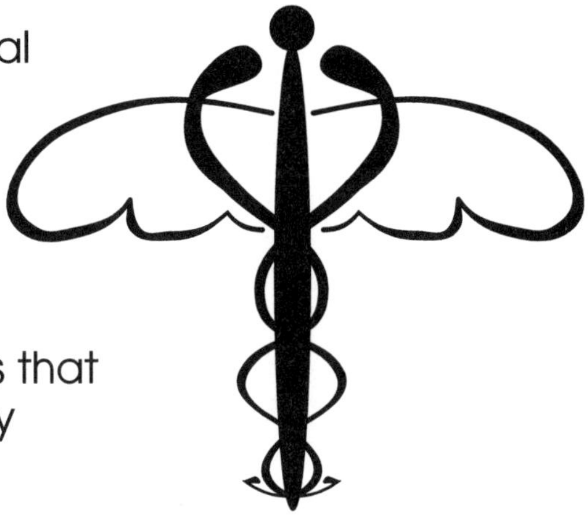

1. diet

a. to make better; to heal

2. cure

b. what a person eats

3. physician

c. sports or other actions that
   are good for the body

4. exercise

d. something that a person gives to another
   person to make him or her well

5. medicine

e. person who helps other people to heal

Choose three words from the list above. Then write a sentence that explains
how each thing or person keeps us healthy.

_____

_____

_____

_____

Name _____ Date _____

In the Marketplace

Directions: ─────────────────────────

Match each word in the left column with its meaning in the right column.

1. cargo   a. to trade one thing for another

2. pirate   b. a person who is owned by another person

3. merchant   c. a place where ships unload what is in them

4. port   d. having a lot of money, land, or other things

5. market   e. a place where people buy and sell things

6. slave   f. what ships carry

7. barter   g. a person who buys and sells things

8. wealth   h. a person who steals what is in ships

Measure and Build

≶**Directions:** ─────────────────────────────────────

Use the Word Bank to help fill in the blanks.

── Word Bank ──

measure	pillar	rows	architect
marble	temple	weighs	cylinder

1. The building in the drawing above is a _____ .

2. It is made of _____ , a kind of stone.

3. This temple has _____ of columns.

4. Another name for a column is _____ .

5. Each column _____ a lot.

6. A column looks like a _____ .

7. A person who draws the plans for a building is an _____ .

8. This person has to be able to _____ well.

Mud Between Your Toes

≥Directions: ————————————————————————

Use the Word Bank to help fill in the blanks.

————————— **Word Bank** —————————

fertile	lacked	delta	flood
silt	canals	dam	

1. The _____ of the Nile River is made of soil that the river has carried.

2. Long ago, the Nile River overflowed each year and left _____ .

3. This _____ soil helped farmers to grow good crops.

4. Even when other people _____ food, the Egyptians usually had enough to eat.

5. _____ carried water from the Nile River to fields.

6. Today, the Nile does not _____ often.

7. The Aswan _____ helps to keep the Nile from overflowing.

Counting and Measuring

Directions:
Use the Word Bank to fill in the blanks.

Word Bank

estimate	practical	rectangle	step
weighed	count	symbols	measure

∩   I   𝕀   ℓ

1. The Egyptians used _____ math, or math that has to do with everyday things.

2. The first pyramids were in the shape of a _____ .

3. They are called _____ pyramids.

4. Some people think that each block of a pyramid _____ $2\frac{1}{2}$ tons.

5. The Egyptians had _____ that stood for numbers.

6. The Egyptians used these to _____ the blocks needed for a pyramid.

7. They also needed to _____ the place where the pyramid was built.

8. People _____ that it took 20 years to build a pyramid.

Bonus: In an Egyptian text, there is a problem about how much grain would be saved if a certain number of cats caught a certain number of rats. People who studied old texts thought this problem was meant as a joke.

© McGraw-Hill Children's Publishing   111   0-7424-1933-9 *Theme-Based Vocabulary Builders*

Science

Making Beautiful Things

Directions: ——————————————————————

Match the word in the left column with its meaning in the right column.

1. bead

    a. a kind of plant, used to make paper

2. reed

    b. a kind of wood, used to make furniture

3. gold

    c. a tall grass that can be used to make baskets

4. papyrus

    d. a kind of soil that can be mixed with water to make cups or bowls

5. lapis

    e. it comes from animal tusks; used to make jewelry

6. cedar

    f. a kind of metal, used to make jewelry

7. clay

    g. a dark blue stone, used to make jewelry

8. ivory

    h. a small piece of glass, wood, or other material with a hole through its middle, sometimes used to make jewelry

All Wrapped Up

⇒Directions:

Match the word in the left column with its meaning in the right column. Use a dictionary if necessary.

1. mummy   a. soft parts of a person's body

2. tissue   b. thick, sticky oil

3. embalm   c. small pieces that fall when wood is cut

4. sawdust   d. a body that has been kept from decay after the person died

5. resin   e. to keep a body from decaying

Analogies

Directions:

Analogies show how words are related.

Complete each analogy.

1. **Rain** is to **spring** as **snow** is to _____ .

2. **Wind** is to **blizzard** as **water** is to _____ .

3. **Warm** is to **summer** as **cold** is to _____ .

4. **Leaves** are to **autumn** as **flowers** are to _____ .

5. **Spring** is to **summer** as **autumn** is to _____ .

6. **Desert** is to **dry** as **coast** is to _____ .

7. **Antlers** are to **deer** as **horns** are to _____ .

8. **Fur** is to **mouse** as **feathers** are to _____ .

9. **Scales** are to **snake** as **skin** is to _____ .

10. **Shell** is to **lobster** as **fur** is to _____ .

© McGraw-Hill Children's Publishing

0-7424-1933-9 *Theme-Based Vocabulary Builders*

Analogies

Directions: ─────────────────────────────

Analogies show how words are related.

Complete each analogy.

1. **Scale** is to **weigh** as **ruler** is to _____ .

2. **Inch** is to **foot** as **centimeter** is to _____ .

3. **Day** is to **week** as **month** is to _____ .

4. **Hour** is to **day** as **day** is to _____ .

5. **Second** is to **minute** as **minute** is to _____ .

6. **Ounce** is to **pound** as **pound** is to _____ .

7. **Round** is to **ball** as **square** is to _____ .

8. **Three** is to **triangle** as **four** is to _____ .

9. **Cylinder** is to **column** as **square** is to _____ .

10. **Curve** is to **circle** as **line** is to _____ .

Analogies

Directions: _____

Analogies show how words are related.

Complete each analogy.

1. **Studio** is to **pictures** as _____ is to the **movies.**

2. **Time** is to **running** as _____ is to the **long jump.**

3. **Boat** is to **sailing** as **bike** is to _____ .

4. **Water** is to **swimming** as **snow** is to _____ .

5. **Paint** is to **painting** as _____ is to **sculpture.**

6. **Breath** is to **horn** as **fingers** are to _____ .

7. **Beads** are to **jewelry** as _____ is to **pottery.**

8. **Piñata** is to **fiesta** as _____ are to **Kwanzaa.**

9. **Turkey** is to **Thanksgiving** as _____ is to **Chinese New Year.**

10. **Fireworks** are to **Fourth of July** as _____ are to **Cinco de Mayo.**

Analogies

Directions:

Analogies show how words are related to each other.

Complete each analogy.

1. **Rock** is to **mountain** as **sand** is to _____ .

2. **Pond** is to **ocean** as **stream** is to _____ .

3. **Trees** are to **forest** as **flowers** are to _____ .

4. **Sand** is to **beach** as **lava** is to _____ .

5. **Grass** is to **marsh** as **moss** is to _____ .

6. **Trees** are to **jungle** as **lichens** are to _____ .

7. **Evergreens** are to **taiga** as **moss** is to _____ .

8. **Rain** is to **rainforest** as _____ is to **tundra**.

9. **Heat** is to _____ as **cold** is to the **Arctic**.

10. **Ice** is to _____ as **rock** is to the **mountain**.

© McGraw-Hill Children's Publishing

0-7424-1933-9 *Theme-Based Vocabulary Builders*

Answer Key

Pretest/Posttest

1. b
2. c
3. b
4. b
5. a
6. c
7. a
8. c
9. b
10. c
11. a
12. c

Page 10

1. stream
2. marsh
3. pond
4. ocean
5. islands
6. glaciers
7. beach
8. dunes

Page 11

1. whale
2. mouse
3. hawk
4. crab
5. turtle
6. snake
7. salamander
8. lobster

Page 12

1. whale, water
2. mouse, land
3. hawk, land
4. crab, both (depending on the kind of crab)
5. turtle, both
6. snake, land
7. salamander, both
8. lobster, water

Page 13

1. whalers
2. images
3. ivory
4. carve
5. scrimshaw
6. folk art
7. museums
8. resin
9. endangered

Page 14

1. f
2. e
3. b
4. h
5. a
6. g
7. d
8. c

Page 15

1. Animals (This answer and the answer to question 2 may be reversed.)
2. Season
3. Animal numbers for two seasons (average)

Page 16

1. circle
2. pie chart
3. segment
4. number value
5. Numbers of mice by season
6., 7. Possible answers may be listed in any combination: late spring, early summer, mid-summer, late summer

Page 17

1. map
2. grid
3. location
4. intersect
5. intersection
6. symbol

© McGraw-Hill Children's Publishing

0-7424-1933-9 *Theme-Based Vocabulary Builders*

Answer Key

Page 18

1. c
2. f
3. g
4. h
5. b
6. a
7. d
8. e

Page 19

1. volcano
2. erupt
3. ash
4. cinders
5. lava
6. vent
7. crater
8. lake

Page 20

1. lizard
2. butterfly
3. brown trout
4. pine marten
5. skunk
6. prairie dog
7. golden eagle
8. salamander

Page 21

1. pueblos
2. resources
3. introduced
4. grassland
5. graze
6. shepherds
7. predators
8. coyote

Page 22

1. land grant
2. census
3. county
4. community
5. acres
6. livestock
7. shear
8. traded

Page 23

1. Number of sheep (This answer may be reversed with the answer to question 2.)
2. Day (This answer may be reversed with the answer to question 1.)
3. Answers will vary.
4. Answers will vary.
5. Answers will vary.
6. Answers will vary.

Page 24

1. feathers
2. scales
3. fur
4. fur
5. feathers
6. skin

Page 25

1. potter
2. pottery
3. clay
4. water
5. coils
6. different
7. symbols
8. fired

Page 26

1. deer
2. rabbit
3. bighorn sheep
4. rattlesnake
5. coyote
6. tortoise
7. scorpion
8. iguana

Page 27

1. prickly poppy
2. dwarf sage
3. barrel cactus
4. smoke tree
5. fluff grass
6. greasewood
7. old man cactus
8. juniper

Drawings will vary.

© McGraw-Hill Children's Publishing

0-7424-1933-9 *Theme-Based Vocabulary Builders*

Answer Key

Page 28
1. heat
2. evaporates
3. gas
4. vapor
5. vapor
6. liquid or solid
7. condenses
8. clouds
9. solid

Page 29
Across
2. three
3. change
5. solid
6. liquid
Down
1. physical
3. chemical
4. gas

Page 30
1. h
2. f
3. e
4. c
5. b
6. d
7. a
8. g

Page 31
1. painted
2. pictographs
3. carved
4. etched
5. petroglyphs
6. explore

Page 32
Pictures will vary. Examples of definitions are
1. traveling in a narrow boat using paddles
2. traveling on a flat structure on water, usually made of wood
3. riding a bicycle
4. exploring and studying caves
5. walking and exploring sometimes wild land
6. crawling up and/or down large rocks
7. taking pictures, often of plants and wildlife
8. finding and studying rocks

Page 33
1. locate
2. origin
3. point
4. coordinates
5. location
6. a stone
7. (3, 2)
8. coordinates

Page 34
1. porpoise
2. mink
3. muskrat
4. woodpecker
5. skunk
6. raven
7. squirrel
8. dolphin

Page 35
Across
2. catfish
3. rabbit
4. otter
7. walrus
Down
1. kitten
3. raccoon
5. eagle
6. cougar

Page 36
1. c
2. d
3. e
4. h
5. g
6. f
7. a
8. b

Page 37
1. d
2. f
3. h
4. g
5. b
6. c
7. e
8. a

© McGraw-Hill Children's Publishing 0-7424-1933-9 *Theme-Based Vocabulary Builders*

Answer Key

Page 39
1. converted
2. alike (This answer may be substituted for question 2.)
3. different (This answer may be substituted for question 1.)
4. centimeters
5. 34 degrees
6. 47 degrees
7. 0 inches
8. 13.8 inches

Page 40
1. d
2. h
3. g
4. e
5. b
6. a
7. c
8. f

Page 41
Maps will vary.

Page 42
1. birch
2. blueberry
3. willow
4. lichens
5. evergreen
6. aspen
7. moss
8. fungus

Page 43
1. caribou
2. wolf
3. weasel
4. lynx
5. grouse
6. wolverine
7. brown bear
8. magpie

Page 44
1. e
2. g
3. f
4. h
5. c
6. d
7. a
8. b

Page 45
1. disease
2. serum
3. malamutes; huskies
4. relays
5. remember
6. route; tundra
7. mushers

Page 47
1. 12:08:45:02 (1981)
2. 12:16:34:39 (1991)
3. 15:10:37:47 (1977)
4. 16:16:27:13 (1977)
5. 11:01:53:23 (1990)
6. 11:02:05:13 (1987)
7. 11:11:41:40 (1988)
8. 11:15:06:00 (1986)

Page 48
Across
2. month
5. decade
7. minute
Down
1. centennial
3. year
4. century
6. weeks

Page 49
1. bark
2. vertical
3. peel
4. regrows
5. sturdy
6. brace
7. stitched
8. dyed

© McGraw-Hill Children's Publishing   0-7424-1933-9 *Theme-Based Vocabulary Builders*

Answer Key

Page 50
1. sphere
2. globe
3. cube
4. cylinder
5. pyramid
6. cone
7. rectangular prism
8. hemisphere

Page 51
1. pattern
2. guide
3. blocks
4. quilt
5. cloth
6. fabric
7. design
8. strips

Page 52
1. recycled
2. scraps
3. stitched
4. pieced
5. expensive
6. exhibit

Page 53
Designs will vary.

Page 54
1. dye
2. minerals
3. plant
4. indigo
5. shellfish
6. ore
7. fabric
8. absorbed

Page 55
1. mixing
2. primary
3. secondary
4. green; secondary
5. secondary; blue
6. violet
7. darkens
8. lightens

Page 56
1. lines
2. vertical
3. horizontal
4. oil
5. palette
6. primary
7. canvas
8. layers

Page 57
1. sun
2. lamps; flashlights
3. energy
4. solar
5. wave
6. bands
7. color

Page 58
1. melting
2. furnace
3. metals
4. minerals
5. discovered
6. potters
7. eyeglasses
8. windows

Page 59
1. cathedrals
2. stained
3. stories
4. symbols
5. pieces
6. mosaic

Page 60
1. cathedrals
2. recall
3. windows
4. pastel
5. public
6. style

© McGraw-Hill Children's Publishing

0-7424-1933-9 *Theme-Based Vocabulary Builders*

Answer Key

Page 61
1. plane
2. polygon
3. vertical
4. parallel
5. next
6. measure
7. dimensions
8. three

Page 62
Across
2. addends
4. equation
6. fraction
Down
1. add
3. estimating
5. quotient
6. factor
7. area

Page 63
Designs will vary.

Page 64
1. jaguars
2. toucans
3. tapirs
4. parrots
5. cougars
6. alligators
7. monkeys
8. opossums
9. iguanas
10. crocodiles

Page 65
1. g
2. c
3. a
4. e
5. h
6. b
7. d
8. f

Page 66
1. system
2. symbols
3. stairways
4. altogether
5. concept
6. calendar
7. astronomy
8. canals
9. calendar

Page 67
1. Mars
2. Saturn
3. Uranus
4. Venus
5. Earth
6. Jupiter
7. Mercury
8. Neptune
9. Pluto

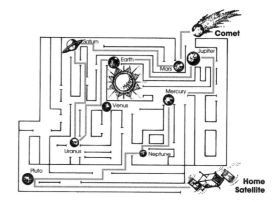

Page 68
1. murals
2. workers
3. industry
4. frescoes
5. national
6. history
7. pride
8. display

Page 69
1. lynx
2. raccoon
3. pheasant
4. walrus
5. otter
6. bighorn sheep
7. beaver
8. Canada goose
9. gopher
10. moose

© McGraw-Hill Children's Publishing 0-7424-1933-9 *Theme-Based Vocabulary Builders*

Answer Key

Page 70
1. e
2. h
3. i
4. j
5. c
6. d
7. c
8. f
9. g
10. b

Page 71
1. fishing—to catch fish with hooks or nets
2. hunting—to find and kill animals for food
3. trapping—to catch animals so one can sell their fur
4. trading—to give on thing in return for another recycled
5. farming—to grow plants or animals for food
6. mining—to dig for gold, coal, or other things in a hole that is under the ground

Drawings will vary.

Page 72
1. natural
2. carve
3. bones
4. antlers
5. weave
6. dollmakers
7. drawings
8. paint

Page 73
1. map
2. direction
3. cardinal
4. compass rose
5. north
6. east
7. west
8. south

Page 74
1. koala
2. dingo
3. wombat
4. crocodile
5. dugong
6. kangaroo
7. wallaby
8. emu
9. penguin
10. platypus

Page 75
1. island
2. continent
3. bush
4. interior; outback
5. graze
6. desert
7. plateaus
8. coral

Page 76
1. stone etchings
2. storytelling
3. pipes
4. bark painting
5. wood carvings
6. boomerang
7. woven baskets
8. didjeridoo

Page 77
1. measurement
2. tall
3. wide
4. straight
5. round
6. converted
7. metric
8. centimeters

© McGraw-Hill Children's Publishing

0-7424-1933-9 *Theme-Based Vocabulary Builders*

Answer Key

Page 78
Across
2. Celsius
6. ounces
7. inches
8. yard
Down
1. liters
3. foot
4. centimeters
5. pints

Page 79
1. deer
2. tiger
3. monkey
4. parrot
5. cobra
6. cattle
7. mongoose
8. sloth bear
9. gazelle
10. elephant

Page 80
1. f
2. e
3. g
4. h
5. d
6. b
7. a
8. c

Page 81
1. e
2. d
3. a
4. b
5. c
6. f

Page 82
1. movies
2. important
3. melody
4. scale
5. theme
6. written
7. invents
8. sitar

Page 83
1. flip
2. turn
3. pattern
4. grid
5. half
6. half
7. same
8. symmetry

Page 84
1. e
2. d
3. b
4. c
5. a
6. j
7. i
8. g
9. h
10. f

Page 85
1. bobsledding
2. skiing
3. figure skating
4. luge
5. hockey
6. snowboarding
7. speed skating

Page 86
1. orbits
2. tilts
3. hemisphere
4. winter
5. hemisphere
6. summer

Page 87
1. h
2. d
3. e
4. g
5. c
6. b
7. f
8. a

Answer Key

Page 88
1. celebrate
2. history
3. community
4. culture
5. candles
6. goals
7. unity
8. feast

Page 89
1. line
2. point
3. labels
4. segment
5. title
6. snow
7. Inches of snow; Day
8. Answers will vary.

Page 90
1. b
2. d
3. e
4. g
5. f
6. h
7. a
8. c

Page 91
1. coat
2. root
3. sun
4. water
5. carbon dioxide
6. flower
7. stem
8. leaf
9. chlorophyll

Page 92
1. record
2. pictograph
3. symbol
4. key
5. The key is one flower equals five plants.
6. The symbol is the flower icon.
7. Answers will vary.
8. The gardener planted lilies, roses, and violets.

Page 93
1. c
2. h
3. e
4. f
5. a
6. d
7. i
8. b
9. j
10. g

Page 94
1. rotates
2. axis
3. equator
4. pole; pole
5. equator
6. equinox
7. spring
8. autumn

Page 95
1. freedom
2. marching
3. ballad
4. nature
5. perform
6. dances
7. piñata
8. fireworks

Answer Key

© McGraw-Hill Children's Publishing

Page 96
1. tennis
2. cycling
3. softball
4. diving
5. basketball
6. sailing
7. baseball
8. volleyball
9. canoeing
10. boxing
Answers to the bonus question will vary.

Page 97
1. e
2. g
3. f
4. b
5. c
6. h
7. a
8. d

Page 98
1. vertical
2. bar
3. bar graph
4. Number of children; Sports
5. basketball, the fourth bar
6. Number of children; Sports
7. baseball, the third bar
8. Answers will vary.

Page 99
1. freedom
2. equal
3. elections
4. capital
5. protest
6. sit-ins
7. boycotted
8. civil rights
9. picnic

Page 100
1. beans
2. turkeys
3. squash
4. ducks
5. corn
6. oysters
7. eel
8. pumpkin
9. geese
10. cranberries
11. mushrooms
12. gooseberries

Page 101
1. d
2. a
3. b
4. c
5. b
6. a

Page 102
1. cycle
2. order
3. seed
4. seedling
5. adult
6. fruit; flowers

Page 103
1. Pilgrims
2. worship
3. *Mayflower*
4. Compact
5. Pilgrims
6. hardships
7. grateful
8. Thanksgiving

Page 104
1. painted
2. family
3. huge
4. real
5. style
6. lines

0-7424-1933-9 *Theme-Based Vocabulary Builders*

Answer Key

Page 105
1. beans
2. grapes
3. olives
4. wheat
5. figs
6. barley
7. hay
8. lentils

Page 106
Pictures will vary.
1. boxing—a competition in which two people wear padded gloves and use skill to fight
2. wrestling—a competition in which two people struggle hand-to-hand to unbalance each other
3. horse racing—horses running, usually around a track, to see which is fastest
4. running—a foot race
5. chariot racing—a competition in which horses pull men in 2-wheeled carts called chariots to see who is fastest

Page 107
1. b
2. a
3. e
4. c
5. d
Sentences will vary.

Page 108
1. f
2. h
3. g
4. c
5. e
6. b
7. a
8. d

Page 109
1. temple
2. marble
3. rows
4. pillar
5. weighs
6. cylinder
7. architect
8. measure

Page 110
1. delta
2. silt
3. fertile
4. lacked
5. canals
6. flood
7. dam

Page 111
1. practical
2. rectangle
3. step
4. weighed
5. symbols
6. count
7. measure
8. estimate

Page 112
1. h
2. c
3. f
4. a
5. g
6. b
7. d
8. e

Page 113
1. d
2. a
3. e
4. c
5. b

Page 114
1. winter
2. rainstorm
3. winter
4. flowers
5. winter
6. wet
7. cattle
8. eagle (or any bird)
9. frog (or any amphibian)
10. otter (or any furry mammal)

Page 115
1. measure
2. meter
3. year
4. month
5. hour
6. ton
7. block
8. rectangle (or square)
9. cube
10. square (or any polygon)

Page 116
1. theater
2. distance
3. cycling
4. skiing (or snowboarding, luge, or other snow sports)
5. stone (or wood)
6. piano (or other stringed instruments)
7. clay
8. candles
9. rice
10. parades (or mariachi bands)

Page 117
1. beach
2. river
3. meadow
4. volcano
5. tree
6. tundra
7. tundra
8. permafrost
9. desert
10. glacier

© McGraw-Hill Children's Publishing

0-7424-1933-9 *Theme-Based Vocabulary Builders*